Wild Yoni Flower

a self love journey

Published by Empressive Expressions, LLC

www.EverythingEmpressive.com

Cover art by Heavenly Jewell's, LLC
Author photo by Ashleen Senexant of Scope Media

For additional information, contact the Publisher at the web address specified above.

First edition.

ISBN: 978-1-7362766-0-0
ISBN: 978-1-7362766-1-7

Printed in the United States of America.

Contents

To my Goddess Ori,

my warrior mama angel,

my future wild flower indigo daughters

and my soul sistren:

may you forever be, "wild, wise and loving."

Wild Yoni Flower:

A Self Love Journey

"Yoni is my sacred center.
Wildness is my core.
My flower feels like silk petals
lightly dipped in coconut oil..."

Part 1 - Wild

I. Wild & Sexy

Journal Entry #1:

It is the morning after the full moon.

Last night I went on a date with a saxophonist.

I wore a tight-fitting dress with no panties and no bra, my three waist beads teasing and tickling my skin.

I felt pretty sexy, scented with my "sacral sexy power" potion.

Little by little, I'm getting my mojo back...

- 5 Nov 2017

∞ ∞ ∞

Naughtiness

Full Moon in Scorpio
And I,
full on scandalous
soaking up all the sexy in the atmosphere,
with no panties on!

Seeking adventure,
I ask the Universe,

"What kind of mischief can I get into tonight?"

Sweet Dreams

I'm having liquid flavored daydreams
and whiskey scented reminiscences.
Slowly sipping spiritual elixirs,
savoring the taste of life.

I'm soulfully LIT!

Getting drunk off of oxygen,
I'm feeeeeeling...
lightheaded.

Overdosing,
intoxicated by the very essence of existence.
Hazy –
head nice boi –
Please,
Please,
Pleeeeeeeeease
Don't
Kill

My
Vibe!

Talking too loudly
and dancing louder
Sashaying down Wynwood
or
life's downtown runway –
I don't remember!

Singing karaoke off key
but still in sync
with the moonlit music
serenading the darkness.

Fading beautifully into the night –
I pass out!

Between dizzying hope
and the corner of ecstasy,
hungover on fantasies,
I stumble and blur realities,
slurring serendipity, all the doo da day!

I swear I'll never indulge again

. . .until the next time that is!

Risqué

The scent of life turned her on.

Time's unmerciful hands made her wet.

Chance

and

Fortune

anticipated her climax

And

from the mystic power

of the mundane,

she came –

hard.

Over

and

over again.

Everything is a stimulus:

trees swaying seductively in the wind,
birds singing sweet nothings,
the sun caressing exposed skin,
its heated kisses tickling her abdomen,
tracing the path from her navel
to her nether,
increasing the private warmth inside,
slowly spreading to regions where the sun don't shine…

The horizon made her do it:
made her slip her fingers into her honey-maker;
made her feel the silky essence of ambrosia on earth;
made her bask in the saturated star showers
of her beloved goddess flower
to fully comprehend the glory of her existence.
The horizon –
made her feel alive.

Just the taste of being made her feverish.
Unwittingly seeking sacral teases from the universe,
she spoons a mouthful
of Caribbean coconut ice cream onto her tongue –
the same color as cum –
and savors its delightful richness;
reminiscing on the last time she indulged in such nectar…

Mellow moments make her moan.

Frenzied acts of quiet impatience

makes her heart race in arousal

like:

sitting in traffic;

mere seconds,

mere inches of volatility,

deliver tremors of sensual thrills hidden in shadows;

the danger of mystery so sexually appealing

she can barely contain the excitement,

the perpetual pleasures derived on the daily

because lately –

everything turns her on.

Including life itself.

She's a walking sensory creature

sentient

to the sensual vibrations

emanating all around her.

Finally embracing her true nature,

she taps into her magic

and surrenders freely to it:

erotic wildness.

Firewater

I got that *firewater* in between my legs.

Each step I take,

Burns

Me

Alive.

I'm surprised,

I don't ignite

as I walk,

sending sparks

from the motion raging deep down below in my insides;

to the contact my feet make once they hit the pavement;

electrifying every innocent bystander within a close radius –

it's a wonder,

my charged atoms aren't attracting more heat!

Causing chemical reactions,

and emitting fevers;

disrupting frequencies of normalcy,

like radiation

due to the atomic bomb
barely diffused in between my thighs...

I
explode inwardly.
Daily.
Silently,
singeing the air with my sexy,
leaving incendiary ashes in the wake of my saunter,
I got that firewater in between my legs.

Combusting internally.
Melting deliciously.
Molten lava pools and simmers
at my center
'til my cup runneth over
releasing rivers of damnation!

Hot
sticky,
sin
seethe under my skin;
soaking my aura in sizzling swag
boiling over in sassy assurance;
power so potent,
I exist in my own sauna.

Humanly humid,

I muse

whether it is possible,

when I pass by,

can people smell the sultry secret exuding
from my perspiration?

I got that *firewater* in between my legs.

All Night Long

Standing in the spotlight
seduced by my own shadow,
I almost made love to the wall…

Struck silly
I spotted me unexpectedly.
Immediately
attracted to my most high spirit,
I snuck glances at myself
all night long.

Blushing but daring
I locked eyes with I and I,
Seductress.
Lingering in front of mirrors
emboldened by my own charisma
I shamelessly flirted with me,
the whole
night
long.

The temptress.
La diosa.
I was immortalized in the music
worshipping tempos
and praise dancing rhythms
summoning a higher power of self,
I got called a Goddess on the dance floor!

And I could see why:

I glowed with the sheen of divinity.
Sweat cascading from my temple like
glorious waterfalls.

Drenched in soul,
I bestowed blessings
with each marvelous hip movement
I,
Miss
Waistline Magician.
casted spells
making sense disappear
pulling arousal out of thin air.

Enraptured,
I became my own victim.

Lured into desire,
my mojo held me perilously close
and refused to let go...

But
I had never felt
more secure
more alive
or more euphoric in my life!

So, I gripped onto me just as tightly
and surrendered to the mystery.
And I and I danced together
so intimately,
all
night
long.

Desire

The tingling begins in my tummy.

Then travels down into my sacred seat.

The warmth then spreads across the middle
and below;
A rush of fervor
slowly melting my insides
like hot candle wax.

Now a pool of liquid collects:
evidence of the internal ether burning.

A mess of me spills onto the sheets,
wetness unrestrained to one spot.

The tingling reverberates
and crescendos
into a pulsating throb.

The need for release so pertinent

and imminent.

My pelvis rises to meet my center.

Heaving thrusts induced

rapid hip mechanics

feeding the friction

fanning the flames

with increased oxygen

yet,

I

can't

breathe.

Nor speak.

Sound coalesces into heat

until all I hear

is

the

throbbing...

Irresistible

I just LOVE a great smelling man!

It makes me weak in the knees
when I pass him by,
just living life,
minding my own business,
only to suddenly get
Soul-Snatched
by the scented essence of GOD!

– *with his ambrosia fine self!*

Wearing the musk of mystery,
midnight,
and seductive magic
all in one.

Oooooweeeeeeee
Come here boi!

What's that cologne you got on?

Damn!

You smell good.

Just like the danger I want to run into.

Senseless once that aroma hits my senses,

all my best laid plans got deferred

and I'm following him like a magnet.

Helplessly entrapped by

the power of the potion.

I pray,

Lawd, help me

and Devil be damned!

I just love a great smelling man.

Yang

Look me in my eyes when I'm fucking you.

Close contact
like we bout to catch a contact
high.

Deeeeep inside.

Energies
transferring
seamlessly,
freely;
our forms collapsing,
shape shifting
into
sweet
silhouettes
of smoke…

But it's thick as fuck in here!

Hot and hazy,
like we puffing on that lie.
I want you to
Pass the dutchie pon the left-hand side
And stick it to me on the right!

Don't you fuck up this rotation.
Give me that sticky
icky
baby.

And
I'll

Give it right back to you,
I
catch that -

reach,

give it
right back to you;
you're
in so deep,
*I'm breathing for you,**

23

I

Inhale...

Exhale...

Pull on it so haaaard,

my lungs hurt!

Well, dammit,

fuck it!

I say,

let 'em burst.

I'll asphyxiate off of you gladly,

granted

your pleasure in HD 3D

is the **_last_** precious sight I see.

So,

look me in my eyes,

when you're fucking me.

*reference to excerpted song lyric, "Crown Royal," Hutson, Lee, JR., Hutson Lee and Scott, Jill (2007).

Masochist

I
just wanna be
ravished.

Savagely

like a rabid beast.

Sink
your teeth,
your limbs,
your meat
in me.

And
don't
let
go.

Grab me.

Grip me.

Choke me.

Grope me,

most inappropriately.

Baby, you have my consent

to assert your alpha

all up

and

down,

in

and

out

and

around

my body.

She's yours to do what you wish.

So, assume illicit intent

because I oblige...

I oblige.

I surrender myself to your mastery.

In sexy S&M fashion:

Sin

and

mischief;

secrets

and

mystery,

I want you to

subdue

and

manipulate me.

Mercilessly.

Sweetly, stifle my cries

and slap me tenderly.

Let me feel the warm sting

of your palm imprint

brandished against my ass!

Spread eagle

and

bent over,

I welcome your force of nature

wildly connecting with my primitive.

Roughly,

ram your desire

deep into my yearning

and

avidly,

penetrate my allure.

Enrapture me in an intense session

of painful pleasure

because I swear,

I have a high threshold for both:

pain

and

pleasure.

And baby,

we're just getting started.

Utopia

Legs open wide ready to receive your gift.
Sensually unguarded,
I lay bare
awaiting the cosmic ecstatic fusion
of our union
as we become one...

Fuck me figuratively.
Literally.
Oppressively,
pressure my pussy
with the power of your powerful private parts.

Parting my flower like the red sea,
you fucking me
is biblical.

Like it was pre-written before.

Divinely predicted,

embedded in scriptures

revealing the testament

of prophetic climaxes.

Gracefully, you glide

your luscious member deep inside

and write your name

all along

and across

my fleshy temple walls.

Let every crevice and fold

within my soul

sing out with praises

ringing the reign

of your holy name...

mmmm...

moans

All praises be to -

he who shall not be named!

Fuck me hard,

soft

tame and wild.

Let me feel the glory of you

within me.

And on top of me.

I oblige to every command you demand
you dominant,
alpha,
epic male
prowling and creeping
out of the wildness that enfolds.

This sexual savagery knows no boundaries
and only you
can subdue me.

Feel free
to let your inner demon loose.

There's no judgment
as we share in sacred sin.

Sinfully, conquer me.

Unequivocally.

Mount me with your fierce masculinity
fucking me
absolutely
and entirely
Complete me.

You, mystic man
merging with me,
enchanted woman.

Your godly phallus
interconnected
with my goddess yoni.
Let us ascend to paradise
and plunge into hell again;
emblazoned in an erotic inferno
immortalizing our passions
fucking into oblivion;
until
eternity
envelopes we
deeply,
intensely,
into the sweet,
lustful darkness.

Sweet Hips

He said,
'I got the sweetest hips this side of the Mississippi!'

'Heaven sent.'

I got him
speaking in tongues,
singing hymns,
and praise dancing the rhythms that flow
like rivered honey from my country backside…
Ready to get baptized!

Swing Low, Sweet Chariot –
I just might send him home to meet his maker!

But if he should go on to glory,
he'll go a happy man;
grinning from ear to ear
singing, *Mississippi Gotdamn!*
- only without the blue melancholy.

I'll have him feeling good
like Nina,
glad to have sampled the holy waters
from my secret well…

Sweet
Glory
Everlasting!

I'll quench his thirst
and redeem his spirit
with erotic melodies
of Hosanna
and
Hallelujah
intertwined
in the rapture of my motion.

Spellbound,
I got him open,
and so awe inspired,
he said,
'he could write a song
about the way I move.'

Well,

I aspire

to inspire him

all

night

long.

Auditioning to become

his new southern staple,

he said,

'My hips

rank up there

with macaroni and cheese.'

Good and hot,

bubbling fresh out the oven –

like good ol' soul food,

I'll comfort him in ALL the right places;

sticking to him in the sweet spots of his soul,

Only won't be no itis fucking with me!

I'll be the

Sugar

Honey

Ice

to his Tea,

blessing him properly.

He betta

bow his head
and clasp his hands
because this year,
I'll be serving Thanksgiving early.

And speaking of miracles,
he placed my hips on the highest pedestal.
Classic idol worship:
he said,
'my hips was up there with
Jordan Retro 11's' –
Good lawd,
he betta quit playing
with all of this blasphemy!

Before I truly return to my heathen ways
and throwback
to the throwback
that I'll throw back on him!
Hoping he can recall his common sense
when I get through
because once I get started…

Oh, goodness gracious!
I'ma do more than lay hands on him!

This is sanctified seduction

christened in the slow and easy
sensual shifts of temptation
I'ma bring him to the paradise
I know
on this side of the Mississippi!

A simple afterlife sweeter than he ever dreamed
I speak to him
in milk and honeyed rhythms,
sacred sounds flowing
like the gentle river running
from my country backside.

'Heaven blessed my hips,'
I tell him.
'So you best believe,
my hips don't lie...'

Nastiness

My mind
lives
in the gutter.

I take refuge in the underbelly of perversion.
So,
pardon,
my freak nature
but I just can't help myself.

Mentally,
I dwell on the outskirts of Skid Row.
Dirty thoughts lurking at my frontal lobe
like that shadowy creep
pleasuring himself in the alley.
So,
while you were
innocently discussing food,
my mind
pictured your lips

wrapped around my fleshy fruit,
sucking out all of its juices
and nutrients;
devouring the stickiness
that drips so sweetly out of me –
but
never mind my nastiness.

Excuse my soiled senses.

I sit delighted by my own filth;
comfortably cloaked in dirt.
Sullied reminiscences
of sweat soaked,
sex scented sheets
reside in the recesses of my subconscious
and I
revel
in it.

Like Oscar the Grouch,
I savor
my sordid sanctuary.
Where every
four letter word
like:

Come here.

Kiss

this.

Your lips

feel good.

Don't stop.

Love that.

Move here.

That spot.

Keep

slow,

then

fast.

DON'T STOP.

Give

more

head

baby.

Damn,

baby.

Blow.

Lick.

Suck.

This

clit.

This

yoni.

DON'T.

DARE.

STOP.

DON'T STOP.

DON'T STOP.

DON'T –

Wait,

What was I talking about?

You see,
elementary vocabulary
gets quickly converted into the illicit
in the vile mental habitat
that governs my secular thinking;
I'm just
so uncouth,
and I don't even try
for discretion.

There's no use pretending,
I'm proud of where I come from.
It is what it is –
my mind:
she stays in the gutter.

II. Wildly Raw: No Fucks Given

Journal Entry #2:

I'm sick of sisterhood honestly.

I feel drained and overburdened by this collective "healing" we are doing or supposed to be doing.

Sometimes it feels like shit is talked to death but still not heard, not felt. And definitely not practiced.

I'm also a bit wary of what I share.

I know I tend to overshare with people too soon. It develops this sense of closeness that seems real but is only temporary. I don't wait long enough to see if the people I'm confiding in are indeed trustworthy and adept at maintaining my secrets. Usually it's a secret-for-secret type of exchange that develops our kinship bonding. But if someone is careless or more free with divulging their own secrets, are they capable of safe-guarding mine?

*Humans are fickle creatures. And unfortunately, with women, instability is consistent. One-minute y'all cool, the next you're not. And it may not even be anything you did or did not do, but rather **an ill-conceived idea** that flourishes out of nowhere and becomes fact.*

I am tired of in-authenticity. I try to be transparent. I also try to pick and choose my battles. Everything ain't worth addressing. Everything ain't a deeper issue. Some shit just needs to be let go.

And some shit needs to be aired out.

But apparently among my "friends" the balance between the two seems to be the source of miscommunication because what I thought had been let go is still an issue. And what I harp on is encouraged to let go. Sigh.

I think I need to embrace solitude more. Not retreat there but embrace it wholeheartedly. I still have the problem of being too available to everyone.

So, I choose me.

I choose to safeguard and honor my own secrets. I choose to hold space with myself. I choose to put me first more often without guilt or shame. I choose to say "no" more often. Or I don't care for this. No matter who agrees/disagrees with it. I choose to be responsible for my own healing. No one else's. I choose to interact with company that can respect those choices.

And I choose to walk my own path authentically and unapologetically whether I have company by my side or not.

- 18 June 2017

∞ ∞ ∞

Candor

Fuck who doesn't have the capability,

the availability

or

the willingness

to see you

for your greatness.

They are unworthy of your grandeur,

undeserving of your presence.

Life is too short for frivolity,

and too long

to remain tethered to bullshit.

So, let those past-expired elements,

gracefully depart from your presence.

Pronto!

Or swiftly,

fall onto your sword –

Fuck 'Em!

Untitled

DON'T DICTATE TO ME HOW TO FUCKING FEEL!

My feelings are not always

convenient

palatable

comfortable

or logical.

Sometimes my feelings don't make any fucking sense!

So while I know

that I *should* know certain things

none of that knowledge matters

when I'm feeling

whatever I'm feeling.

Thanks for reminding

To think though…

Male Entitlement

Male entitlement makes me so damn sick!

Don't summon me
like I'm some dog!

Beckoning me with sweet condescension
is not appealing
nor sexy,
I have no desire to come to you.

I'm also not a doll.
No,
I don't want to plaster a smile
on my face,
or
perhaps, I do
just not for you
I'm tired of faking it
to protect your frail ego anyways.

Soooooo,

what part of not interested,

do you not understand?

My lack of participation in this verbal assault –

ahem, excuse me –

exchange,

makes no difference to you, huh?

sucks teeth

Okay.

Le sigh.

Why

do you need to inquire of my marital status

to bestow an insincere compliment?

Yes, I'm married

to my damn self.

Or

happily, single

and not looking.

Choose whichever answer

that will aid in your quick disappearance

because they both apply.

Anyways,

Mister man

I'm not flattered

by your annoying,

aggressive

unwanted

attention.

It's quite off putting.

So,

quit intruding my space –

uninvited,

then expecting me to be

apologetic

for rejecting your advances.

With all due respect,

Fuck you sir.

Signed,

That bitch

you ultimately think I am anyways.

Bittersweet (Dedication to him, and him...and him too)

What hurt you?

It hurt when he dismissed me.
It hurt when he left.
It hurt when he reentered
and then
when he left –
again.
It hurt when he broke promises;
when all he had to offer was lip service;
when he lied,
lied,
lied;
and then lied some more.

It hurt when I believed him.
It hurt when I forgave him.
It hurt when he forgot.

It hurt when I remembered.
It hurt when I defended him
I protected him
I uplifted him.
It hurt when he took me for granted;
that he didn't even try,
when he delivered excuse
after excuse
and when I accepted them.
It hurt when I rejected him.
It hurt when I stopped caring.
It hurt when I grew cold
and he was silent –
so was I.

It hurt when I didn't recognize who I was anymore.

But
then
one day
it hurt less.
I healed more.
And soon,
I'm hoping
it won't hurt at all anymore.

Forewarning: I Am NOT the One

Intonations of intentions

incubate internal energies

in an impenetrable force-field of invisibility

and

intensely elevated intuition

ensures the aura

is guarded securely –

in other words,

I'm

Unfuckwithable!

Toting crystals and purple pistols,

at first glance,

perhaps,

I don't seem armed and dangerous.

But

my gangsta

lurks menacingly beneath the surface.

Silently concealed in sweet smiles
and twinkling eyes,
my sinister insidiousness
lies in wait
strategically plotting on unsuspecting souls
deceptively cloaked behind my mellow.
Whether emanating that carnal power
or oozing in sacral
chakra
savagery,
you have no idea
the type of *heat* that I'm packing.

So beware.

Don't let my radiance mislead you.
I **am** light.
But I am also deeply entrenched
in the trenches of my darkness.
Thus, the damage I could impart in
subtle shadows,
swiftly mar hearts
before beings even realize
they've been touched by doom.

The mystery of my intrigue

overshadows the depths to my madness.

Which,

typically, is how I prefer it

but as my mama says:

'You betta recognize crazy when you see it.'

And I am authorized to carry crazy.

Daily.

Fully loaded with an extra clip;

to protect my joy at all costs

I am unafraid

to unleash

the wrath

of the fierce wild woman;

To set fire to some shit

then walk away

unfazed by the chaotic ruin

disintegrating at my back,

ever so calmly

Waiting to Exhale.

So don't come for me.

Because it can just as easily be "fuck you"

followed by a loving "Namaste,"

as I cross myself

to exorcise the demons

that dared to cross my path

– at their misfortune –

thinking my Zen meant naiveté

when my innocence is only in the intentions

to be free of injury

and not cause harm to another.

But I will strike if need be.

Holy, yet deadly,

I practice peace

but I'm always primed at the ready

to defend serenity for my soul's sake

'By

Any

Means

Necessary.'

So just don't fuck with me.

And it's all love.

One love.

Always.

∞∞∞

I'm tired of feeling like ...

*hope is the wrong choice to make
because it hasn't yet been worthwhile
for me to get my hopes up...*

∞∞∞

So, What If It Hurts

Right in the process of my own evolution,
becoming better must mean losing innocence
and it's so unfortunate.
I regret that past experiences
leave me with such little hope for the future,
when I used to expect so much more.

Now I fear getting my hopes up;
because it makes more sense to just be realistic,
there's less chance for disappointments.
I'm afraid to really dream anymore…

But so what if it hurts?
Is this newfound practicality,
this philosophy for playing it safe
justifiable for denying the most optimistic pieces of me
because the pain becomes too much to bear sometimes?
Won't it still hurt anyway?
Shrugs.
So what if it does?

I am so strong.

I can withstand
and have withstood
more than I would have thought myself capable of.

But sometimes it feels like the littlest thing will break me.

And a part of me wants to fall apart.

I no longer want to hold it all together;
to simply move on.
I wanna grieve for the loss of me;
for the girl I used to be;
for the woman I thought I was becoming.

I long for her innocence;
for her naivete;
for her willingness to risk it all
for a concept she believed in
even when it caused her suffering…

So what if it hurts right?

Growing pains.
When things change and yet stay the same.

I'm glad I changed

and yet I wish I wasn't so different.

I wish I felt less powerless.

Like if thinking is destiny,

why haven't my thoughts created the reality
I originally sought before?

What happened to all my imaginative visions?

What's this convoluted mental space where I now reside?

It doesn't make much sense here

And this isn't where I wanted to be…

Wishful thinking:

thinking I could control what happens to me.

I mean what do you do when the sky is falling
down around you?

When the pieces continue to cut you,

long after the dust has permanently settled?

When no amount of storm preparation
and protection is enough?

So, what if it hurts?

I don't want to be reactionary anymore.

I want to actually decide my fate.

But there's so much more beyond my grasp,

so much unpredictability,

how can you ever be sure about anything or of anyone?

You can't.

So I struggle with being fully present.

Engaging in connections I feel sooner or
later will cease to matter,

since that has long been the pattern

and old habits die hard...

Happiness is a state of being I have to work hard to maintain.

But I miss those blissfully ignorant days

where wisdom didn't cost me my optimism.

And soft skepticism wasn't so damn seductive.

Reluctant to openness,

it's easier to retreat to reclusive solitude

even when the burden of loneliness becomes
too heavy to bear sometimes.

So what if it hurts?

The pain hasn't yet broken me.

It's an indicator that I still exist

I'm still alive

I still endure.

I still survive even when I don't want to,

I still move forward.

Getting better despite the occasional relapse,

I'm

Still

Here.

So, what if it hurts...

Bring it!

Too Much

Have you ever started to feel like the world
is just too much sometimes?

Like you know that there is good present.
And the sun is shining
and you ate today
and you're breathing
and you're here.
But not *here*.
And you don't want to be here
for the moment;
until the moment of heaviness passes.
Because it just feels like too much of...
Everything.

How is it alright but not alright?

The irony of comedy and tragedy:
laughing, crying faces
taunting,

mimicking,

performing

the duplicity of reality;

the surreality of life.

Because we all wear a mask, right?

Sometimes for no reason at all,

or maybe for all the reasons we refuse to mention,

it just feels like;

it just becomes:

too much.

Lip Service

I've pretty much learned
that people talk just to talk.
Word is not bond.
Intentions
are not
indicative of commitments
or
of actual action.

Promises are simply platitudes
haphazardly administered
because they appear pretty in the moment.
There's no substance.
They're petty provisions
ill-equipped to properly fix shit.

Forget the principle
of saying what you mean,
people often forget half the jargon
they impart

as soon as it

impulsively tumbles out of their mouths.

Oddly infatuated with the sounds

of their own voices;

people proclaim authenticity

even when they have nothing

of relevance,

purpose,

or honor

to say.

But there's value in offering solidarity,

I suppose,

even if

it's only hollow...

It's Hard Being The Strong One

It's hard being the strong one most of the time.

People forget
that you cut
and you bleed
and you tire.

Because it's customary
seeing you so tirelessly
uphold the world.

You're so great at supporting everyone else,
they forget
you need support too;
that you also have burdens to lay down;
that you also bend
and break
and crumble.

They ignore the fault lines in your foundation

because your stillness says you're sturdy.

Your stoic silence shows no sign of frailty

so, they applaud your bravery;

forgetting that your strength doesn't prevent
you from suffering,

it only makes you better at hiding it.

Long live the strong silent type.

I pray,

our silence doesn't suffocate us.

Lawd please help us,

because it's hard.

Secrets

I'm very good at hiding my pain.

I'll plaster a Stepford-wife smile
on my beautifully chiseled,
artfully poised
mask.

Bearing secrets barely buried below the surface,
my grin widens
as I ever so slyly
challenge the world to perceive me
as anything less
than okay.

I'll hug you fiercely,
hiding the gaping wounds I harbor.
Wincing internally
as each embrace
cuts deep into the soul of me.
I'll hold on

for just a second too long;
clutching desperately onto hope
and solace.

But as we disentangle from each other's arms
and my mute pleas for help go unnoticed,
I'll gather myself once more
square my shoulders
and straighten my stance,
like I didn't just almost crumble under the
enormous
invisible
load
no one sees me carrying.

I will look you dead in the eye
with an intense gaze
screaming
Get Out.
Subliminally sending furtive glances
to signal
the mess I've made,
silently,
bleeding all over the place.

I survey scenes so gracefully,
it shrouds any warning issuance

alluding to

the gut-wrenching aches I wrestle with

or

the persistently dull head throbbing

that triggers my imperceptible eye twitching.

Loss and loneliness

stay suppressed in tears

that know better than to fall;

as my pupils plead

to be sincerely seen

before I blink –

breaking the spell

and sinking further into the Sunken Place;

the darkness cloaked behind my sight

mistaken for a beautiful air of mystery.

Because I will never tell:

where I've been;

what I saw;

what I went through;

how I feel.

I'm very good at hiding my pain.

Confession

Sometimes,
I fantasize about my own death.

Sometimes, it's at my hand.
Other times, it's a freak accident.
In any case,
I envision it vividly.
and with each scenario,
I think about the impact
my loss will or won't make;
what people will say,
and whether or not
they're saying those things
because they mean them
or simply, because I'm gone.

That would imply, of course,
that what's said is positive.
Would it really be though?
I don't know.

I've thoughtfully considered suicide
more than a few times,
and have only hesitated
because of my pride.

I couldn't bear the thought
of being seen as less than –
although I wouldn't be here to see it.

I'm too prideful to quit
even when I'm too tired to continue;
too defeated in spirit,
I must keep on living.
It's the only thing I know how to do,
even when I don't know how to do it.

It is said that pride goeth before the fall…
Oh, the irony.
I keep on falling.
And falling.
And falling…
into nothing.

Unicorn

I'm not a fucking unicorn!

I'm not some fictive fantasy
existing in dreams
and storybook fables –
I mean,
just because I'm mystical
doesn't make me some mythical creature.

Yea, I'm special.
But
I'm
Fucking
Real.

I've got baggage.
I've been damaged.
I too, am a work in progress
in the process of healing.
But yes,

I am also powerful.

But not on some unrealistic-comic book-

supernatural-type strength.

But, like:

I wake up.

I get up,

and move with purpose.

Despite the pitfalls that impede my journey.

Despite the agony.

And the uncertainty.

And the occasional crippling loneliness.

And the internal guilt,

shame

and irrational conflict –

I fucking exist

in this dimension.

I am not a fucking unicorn!

My life ain't all rainbow Skittles,

cloudless days,

and infinite sunshine.

You think, cuz I've learned to smile

during the storms,

that I haven't been struck by lightning?

That I haven't been shook by thunder?

That I haven't drowned before

in the torrential downpour

of

chaos,

stress

or

those fucking biblical floods

of depression and damnation?

Shit,

I built my own ark

– brick by brick –

and wasn't no two by two

to keep me company.

Nor any disciples to witness

my resurrection;

my truth doesn't come so neatly gift wrapped

in instructive allegory –

it's more complicated than that.

I'm tired

of being looked at in awe.

Placed on this imaginary pedestal of magic,

told over

and over again

how extraordinary I am,

only to be slandered with insults

for having the audacity

to be extra

different.
Their illusive bubbles bursting
upon realizing
my ass really does defy
the picture perfect pristine character
they had envisioned.

Or rather,
badly scripted.

Cue villainous laugh

What a wicked plot twist
to the happily ever after I guess.
But,
once upon a time,
I was never ordinary,
remember?

I'm not a myth.
I have a history
and it's beautifully ugly.
My past does not come painted in pretty pastels
and my present
radically differs
from the rose-colored visions you donned
when you grew enchanted

with the *idea* of me.

Shit,

I don't much like the color pink anyways.

I don't fly.

I'm not pure.

Nor innocent.

I don't have some magnificent horn –

I'm not a fucking unicorn.

But I am fucking amazing!

And just because you don't know what to make of me

or

couldn't possibly comprehend:

what I am;

who I am:

this glorious,

untamed,

liberated

individual

boldly,

existing in front of you,

doesn't make me

any

less

real.

Or my story
any less compelling.
You just don't deserve to know it.
You're far too busy,
still playing make believe...

∞∞∞

Journal Entry # 3:

It's okay to grieve.

Even to wallow a bit if it means getting to the other side of peace and acceptance.

*What's <u>**not okay**</u> is to claim peace and internally be at war.*

I have to be gentler with me and stop blaming myself for all the shit that goes wrong when I know I've been trying my best.

It ain't like I don't give a fuck. I give too many fucks! Lol

<u>***I deserve to be here.***</u>

I am worthy. I am a good person and I deserve to be happy.

I need to stop thinking misery is my due or cosmic/karmic penance. Fuck that!

I am love, loving and loved.

- 18 Jan 2018

∞∞∞

Part 2 - Yoni

III. Yoni Love & Self-Discovery

Journal Entry # 4:

Dear Journal,

I want a love so plentiful that it just keeps overflowing abundantly.

We never get thirsty. We never get depleted. I spill into him, spilling into me. It's an endless cycle of nourishment.

Sometimes I fear I am being naïve. And that such a profound love is just mere fantasy. But then I feel the yearning in my spirit. The love in me calls out to that great love pending. It's out there. He's out there. I can feel it.

But what am I willing to give up to get to where I need to be? Where I want to be?

I give up emotional burdens, old scars, fleshly temptations, casual carnal delights, physical pleasures without deep soulful connections; a projected future with you know who…

I am seeking communion with a mate I can journey with on all levels. The one I can walk through life with.

I am committed to him. I know he is on the way…

- 3 May 2017

∿∽∾◌◖

Profound Love

I want a love so profound
that constellations
boast new birth patterns of nebula
just to saturate the night sky
with intricately lit expressions
of the affections
written inside my heart.

I want a love so profound
that the heavens reverberate in cosmic ecstasy
at the miraculous legacy
brought forth in bonded bliss;
that ancestral spirits
rise up to personally commend me
on successfully achieving
life's greatest mission,
and then graciously bestow upon me
their most coveted blessings.

I want a love so profound

that time has no meaning.
Forever is only a moment to us
swiftly spontaneous,
yet freely unbounded
transitioning from zenith
to zenith;
that even death
only postpones the longevity
of the greatest love story ever known.

I want a love so profound
that history rewrites itself.
Our gift will be the key
to unlocking humanity's treasured,
but diminishing beauty.
Peace on earth
will reign in perpetuity
as a tribute
to the communion
convened between we.
Our commitment so universally transformative
that the world has no choice
but to stop and take notice
and then,
emulate its richness.

I want a love

So

Profound,

that it stands as an exemplary testament

of the absolute best

that this life

has to offer.

Relationship Goals

I want that
Pinky and the Brain partnership
where our daily mission is to:
'try to take over the world.'

We,
two forces unstoppable,
a dynamic duo
in sync seamlessly,
where he thinks
and
I move.

And vice versa.

Operating fluidly in tandem
as
one
powerful
entity,

we vividly unify
as essential complements:
epitomizing the sun
and the moon.

I want that
Jack and Jill bond
where together we share the same pitfalls of life.
The same way Jill came tumbling
after Jack broke his crown,
without hesitation,
I shoulder his pain
never allowing my king
to bear his burdens
alone.

I want to be his peace;
the comfort he seeks
to restore balance
when the outside world
endeavors to upset his sanity.
I
uplift him
effortlessly,
and he too
shields me
in affectionate support;

giving me

all I want

and

need

his favorite pastime;

protecting me

from unnecessary

suffering and pain.

I am finally at ease with another soul;

trusting him absolutely with my heart.

I want the freedom

to be me;

for him to love me

just the way that I am

for *who I am*

and not

for who he expects me to be.

I am not some cookie cutter mold

he tries to reconfigure

to fit the superficial image

of the ideal wife

he had envisioned –

but, rather

his wife

because I break the mold of everything he imagined possible;

embodying a reality far greater
than he had ever dreamed.

I want magic!
Pixie dust and wishes granted by genies;
a spellbound love
enchanted by romanticism
and mystery;
deeply rooted
in Happily Ever After,
despite the sobering impact
of significant real-life obstacles.
Our union
will bear the imprint
of sweet fairy tale kisses,
where looking at him
instigates random outbursts of song
boasting extravagant
melodic
joy;
declaring the impossible
possible,
(it's possible)
because
just by existing,
he proves that dreams do indeed come true.

Only when I close my eyes,

he doesn't disappear into fictive storybook land.

No abstract fantasy,

this man lives

and breathes.

A multidimensional

complete

being;

enriched by an in depth

textural passion

deeply outlining the touch of his skin

affirming the truth

of my forever in the flesh;

as nightly,

I sense his presence by my side,

and daily,

I awake to the reality that

He

Is

Mine!

…

One day.

Kismet

When we embraced,
our skin cells sighed in contentment.
Partial particles reconnected with lost atoms
as molecules of memory regenerated our former selves,
triggering an instant reaction of indivisible wholeness.

When the membranes of our metaphysicality met again,
links of you bonded with chains of me
and the pieces of matter dispersed among the universe
reassembled our previous reincarnations 'til an inexplicable
chemistry reignited once more…

Reunited and it feels so good.

I knew you before I knew you.
We were familiar once,
we were known.
And I remember you then
as I remember you now,
since the soul holds onto what the mind tries to forget.

However, loving you is instinctual.
Intuitive messages encrypt your lips in a tender solace.
Cosmic kisses
send signals to my mind's eye
of fated connections
predestined
to collide in epic greatness;
of intertwined twin spirits;
reawakened yearnings of ancient sacral sensations;
such intimacies shared on a psychic plane.

When you touched me,
my soul returned
from the many journeys
it voyaged across time infinity
And it,
I,
We
came back home;
home to you.

Everything had to happen how it did
just so we could return right back here
to this spot,
in this place,
in this moment,

right now.

It all makes sense now doesn't it?
Why we are here?
Coming full circle
back to us.

Fate

We met each other one week and many moons ago.

Where dozens of lifetimes transpired
in just one night.

And transformations
and completions
came full circle
to meet this connection
we fostered
long before
we first introduced ourselves.

Déjà vu
Coincidence
Cosmic intervention –
whatever this is,
was,
will be ..
Thank the universe, we're here now.

First Impression

He said he saw joy in me.
That's what attracted him to me
in the first place.

He saw my light,
and said,
"I need that.
I need that joy
and that love in my life."

I keep beaming.

Smiling as he describes my brightness.
Blushing so hard, my cheeks hurt.
Silently glowing in spirit,
the intensity grows
as the radiation from his aura
infuses with my own.

He's so energy generous

and he doesn't even know it!

He said,
I looked happy,
so free.

So, like a magnet,
he was drawn close
compelled to inquire
of the genius he was witnessing.

Mysterious.

I remember his eyes:
gentle but probing;
lit with a quiet strength,
I secretly
flushed under his gaze,
excited.

He said he saw joy
when he first saw me.

And I believe him.

But I also wonder,
if what he saw,

was a reflection
of the magic
he too possesses?

Because I see stars when I look at him,
infinitely shining;
I see:
inspiration.

Intimacy

Strumming my pain with his fingers...
Killing me softly with his song...*

He's

killing

me

softly

with this mentally titillating madness.

This

lyrical conniption

of thoughtful intercourse;

he entered

his scholarly instrument

deeeeep

inside

of my brain.

Seducing my internal contemplations

with his virile intelligence,

he telepathically,

deflowered my aura.
Unchastely leaving his mental mark behind:
a special stain signifying his presence;
now my train of thoughts are scattered
flooded with wicked distractions.

My perception will never be the same.

He
parted
his
lips
and
sexy innocence
tongue-kissed knowledge
in a breathtaking move
that defied social pretention.
And
all taboos
against
public displays
of affection,
because
it's difficult
to control
how I'm
affected

in public.

I
experience
multiple
eargasms
oral spasms
and psychological wetness.

Sharing space,
and
exchanging energies
with this individual,
he now exists in my chakras;
wonderfully
defiling
my essence.

Inducing climatic expressions
in intimate,
scintillating conversations –
This man!
is killing me softly...

*Killing me softly with his song...**

*reference to excerpted song lyric, "Killing Me Softly With His Song," Fox, Charles, Gimbel, Norman, and

JAIYE EMPRESS

Lieberman Lori**(1972).

**Lori Lieberman has not been officially credited for co-writing the lyrics, but her invaluable contribution and inspiration for this classic song title does not go unrecognized nor unacknowledged.

∞∞∞

Journal Entry #5:

I am going to be a radical lover.

As a life partner, I will be:

loyal

supportive

compassionate

patient

loving – I will extend myself to aid in his spiritual growth

tranquil – I will provide for and be his peace

encouraging

I will affirm and speak life into him

committed

passionate

open and transparent

soothing

honest

I will fight <u>with</u> him not against him.

I will love him fiercely with everything in me.

…

I want a partner that is committed to going through the trenches of life with me. I want to sit with someone and share my soul in peaceful silence.

I want our spirits to hold hands with one another in the shadows.

- 13 November 2018

∞∞∞

He Says My Laughter Brings Freedom

He said my laughter brings freedom.

Expressing my glee naturally,
summoned forth an instinctive urge;
this
deeper calling in him
to suddenly discover
all of the missing pieces
to life's greatest puzzle.

He swore,
all of the answers
and then some,
could be found
somewhere hidden
inside the timbre of my chuckle.
So he searched the sound and received salvation.

He said my laughter brings freedom.

So when I bellowed loudly,
candidly,
with my joy,
he learned new ways of being.

He envisioned possibilities
previously deemed unimaginable,
developing a sense for the fantastical,
he released all preconceived meanings
of reality;
surrendering to the beauty
of the unknown.

When I laughed,
he saw the sweetest of adventures.
He heard promises of wild abandon.
He felt truly vibrant,
the most alive!

So,
I
let loose
a wicked fit
of unrestrained giggles;
conjuring hope

from

way down

in the wells of my belly,

reverberating love

from the very fiber

of my being,

and

I

set

him

free.

$\mathcal{H}e$

He has a laugh that feels like sunshine.
A smile just as bright
and radiant
as the full moon.

Similarly,
I'm always comforted by his spirit,
lit up on the inside by his kindred glow.
Washed anew
and held steady by the low tides
flowing from his heart to mine;
his sheer brilliance tickles me on the inside.

He has a gentleness.
A tender impact
that moves you
yet doesn't overwhelm.
He moves lightly,
softly,
peacefully

like a gazelle.
Wakanda grace
distinctive in his gait,
I don't question
the sovereignty of his presence,
so majestic
I'm blessed
to receive entry into his kingdom.

Because it was written...

He has a laugh that rivals sunshine.
A smile just as bright
and dazzling
as the full moon.

His brilliance soaks up all my shadows
and touches all of my hidden places
lighting me up from the inside.

He opens me up
to a brightness
that my life
didn't know it was missing.

(Future) Him

I ain't even tripping,
cuz I've already fallen for him.

But then,
he picks me back up again.

You see,
my future husband
elevates me
while also holding me down.

Rooted in his rib
I am anchored
as his base protection,
I shelter his heart
as he safeguards mine.

My mind
is blown
by the moment

of realization that

he is

the prophetic vision

I manifested

forever ago,

tomorrow.

Though yesterday, I didn't yet know him,

I see him clear as day presently in our future.

So, I ain't too much worried about what's
not going on right now.

I'm single, but spoken for.

I've already fallen in love with the one who's on his way...

My Soul

My soul craves independence.

And adventure.

And change.

Thrills,
feels,
love.
Love.

And love.

Epiphany

I didn't know how
to want what I wanted
without giving away
all the pieces of me to obtain it.

And that's why it eluded me.

I shouldn't have to give away *me*
to gain something else.

Because I am everything.

And anything else is
extra.

I am love.

Thus,
I am the greatest power of all.

I can overcome any fear
and any obstacle
because
I am powerful.

I am love.

I am more than enough.

Untouchable

You can't hurt me –
I'm untouchable!

Unreachable,
you're reaching for a magic
well beyond your grasp.

Desperately extending fingertips
that were never meant to caress this beauty.
Aspiring to heights unattainable,
like Icarus
with a faulty wingspan,
ill-equipped to provide the flight ascension
to actually embrace my light.

Pitifully grabbing at intangible brilliance;
clutching at whimsical longings of hopes unfulfilled;
free-
faaaaaaaaalling ...

Empty handed.

Be careful what you wish for.

Pictured above:
picturesque visions
of incredible,
indescribable feelings;
a lovely, enchanted Luna like spectacle
illuminating your life in ways unimaginable;
a grandeur not meant to be held
only beheld in awe,
admired from afar,

though it's no secret that you want me.

Sympathetic to your agony,
I may be
but no –
I am not sorry.

I'll remain shrouded in sweet distant obscurity
proudly posted on my pedigree
smugly beaming;
gleeful with the inherent knowledge
that try as you might –
you can't hurt me.

Because it's obvious:

I'm untouchable!

∞∞∞

Journal Entry #6:

When it comes to romance, I want to be very clear:

I plan to befriend my future lover and life partner.

I plan to genuinely hold space for them and they will do so for me. Nothing I request of him will be considered too much because he will do everything within his power to add to my happiness. He will see me, accept me, uplift me, edify me. He will actively work <u>with</u> me to ensure our bond is healthy and strong and durable. He will be open, humble, compassionate, gentle, kind. He will listen and respond effectively, expressively. He makes sure that us communicating smoothly is top priority.

I wish for a mature individual, spiritually sound, grounded and guided, who is wholeheartedly committed to mutual growth and healthy love. That person will be my life partner. We will build on a solid foundation of respect, friendship, kindness and loyal commitment. We will trust one another. We will support one another.

This future partner will be a believer in justice. They will advocate for those unable to do so for themselves. They will have respect for all life. They will be mindful of how their thoughts and actions effect the world around them. They will have a big, open heart and a deep, beautiful soul. They will be unafraid to feel deeply or to allow those feelings to guide them. They will reflect/mirror the best parts of me. They will inspire me to do and be better.

We will do and be better together.

My soul needs understanding and freedom. The inner me needs a mate that sees me for who I am and lets me just be.

I need a soul who makes a valiant effort to connect with my soul. That's where everything stems. If we don't have that, the core substance is missing.

Speak to my soul. Move my spirit. Cradle my heart.

Be wild and free with me.

Be still with me.

Just be with me.

- 12 March 2018

∞∞∞

I twirl, swirl, dance...

flirt, kiss and flutter away...

∞∞∞

IV. Yoni Power: My Sacred Sensuality

Journal Entry #7:

I am my own soulmate.

"I stand by me holding my hand firmly through good and bad times. I support me without judgement."

I am connecting to the soul in me and self-mating.

I am my own soulmate.

- 25 March 2018

∞ ∞ ∞

Tumbao

*Esa negrita tiene tumbao...**

Sweet percussive sounds announce her presence
as she walks with the syncopation of ancestral drums
embedded in the curvaceous spine
of her sinewy backside.

Dale mami,
ayyyyyyy!

It's
A
Full
Moon
Rising.

Mucha magia que hay en sus caderas.
Cascading craters explode cuando te muevas.
Todo el mundo te mira y fascina
Así que, no pare tu ritmo mami

Keep striiiiiding
in your queenly stride;
strutting with the force
that shakes this Earth
ahora
y para siempre.

Esssssso es!

Esa negrita tiene tumbao.

Hear her heartbeat echo into eternity
with every footstep
because her pasión por la vida is that deep.
Living out loud is the only way she can move,
more so led by the moon in a magnificent direction.
Sus movimientos so deliberate
and poignant,
the world is struck mute.

Impressed by her impressive volumen –
so boisterous,
men
and
women
fall victim
to the rhythmic sensualidad

residing inside her soul.
Helplessly captivated por su poder,
porque infinite ache tiene ella.
Ase!
Y azuuuuuuucar!
She has it all.

Birthed by la Luna,
celestial badness blesses her beauty
as night shades her spirit
shrouding her essence in beloved mystery.

Who is this –
Quien es
esa divina?

Howling wild
and gliding gloriously into her greatness.
Eclipsed by black girl magic
Y la brujería,
Quien es
this lunar goddess?
This seductive enchantress,
stealing hearts and snatching souls
in a swift sultry eyed second,
unrepentant for the sacred possessions she seizes?

Esa negrita es

mi madre,

mis hermanitas

mija futura bonita;

Ella es me.

La emperatriz

Y tiene todo el tumbao

Y más, y más, y más!

Esa negrita tiene toda:

La energía,

la salsa

y escencia divina,

el amor.

I,

she,

we

are

rhythm.

Míranos

Y escucha bien.

Eso, mamita, esssssso!

refers to "La Negra Tiene Tumbao" sung by Celia Cruz.

Enchanted

The ludic sounds of the drums
invite me to embrace spontaneity.
So, with wild abandon,
I let my youthful spirit break free
and dance in gleeful mischief.
The rhythm flows through my veins
like an eternal spring
and as long as the music plays,
I feel,
as if I could live
forever.

Dance

I want to dance!

I want to escape all feelings,
and move uninhibited.
Senseless.
Until my pheromone laced sweat wreaks havoc in the air;
my dangerous sensuality
free flowing loose,
seized by the moment,
enticed by freedom
freely unfolding in limbs undefined
movements unrefined…

Hot blooded desire
courses liquid fire in my veins
burning alive.
Scorched by tempered rhythms,
I must get rid of this
too muchness.
Just touch me

if you dare,

be consumed by my fire.

I want to destroy.

Sweet destruction in my waistline;

powerful hips deconstruct

and rebuild kingdoms

at the slight

and twist

and dip

and rooooll

and sway

of her sly gracefulness.

Baby girl bends

waaaaaay

down

low,

killing souls.

Legs of thunderous might

locked in erotic intensity

fleeting to blissful oblivion

of honorable mentions

fading into dark infinity

where matter doesn't matter

and forever feels like four seconds...

But,

no matter how brief,

let me feel this.

All of this.

Everything

and

nothing

all at once,

sensations running amok

as instinct

commands attention

and primal passion

takes full control;

on high alert;

acutely on edge,

I'm ready to fight

or fly to ecstatic heights...

I'm not sure yet.

Could be either,

might be both.

But hell bent on releasing this rage,

my adrenaline kicks into overload,

it's time to activate survival mode:

I *need*

to dance.

∞∞∞

I burn slowly...

Ignite me

and

I'll dance for you.

Softly collapsing in ashes

all around you,

I'll surround you

with my delicate embers

trembling

from the glowing heat you instill,

when you set me aflame.

Kindle me softly,

and

I will seduce you.

I will deeply penetrate your essence

with my presence

'til you can't help but to breathe me in.

I will tickle your tonsils,

and entice your taste buds

sensual teases enrapturing your senses

so, soon

you will be consuming all of me.

I flush with excitement

at the thought of you watching.

Slyly, I swirl

suspended in space

airily floating as if

in a trance;

wafting

in hypnotic saunter

as you stare,

transfixed;

serenaded by my corporeal song.

Move with me.

Let us fall

into the elements.

You be my fire,

and I,

your earth.

Organically entangled

and also, free.

Free-spirited,

forged in finite forever's

no need for extinguishing this sensation;

just let it

fade away,

all

on

its

own...

Who am I?

I'm your...

Incense

∞∞∞

Lovechild

I say to my future daughter:
You were conceived
in the middle of the dancefloor.

A lovechild inspired in impulsive actions,
you sprung from the magic
of a moment so momentous,
so celebratory
I praise-danced your presence
before your very existence.

I mated musically with the spirits
to produce your immaculate conception.

Seduced by the sounds of sensuality
I deliberately called you forth
from the joyful depths of the hazy darkness.

Possessed by secular rhythms,
your mother traded her innocence for powerful pelvic thrusts

and fluid hip rotations;
liberated limbs
free flowing in frenzied movements
engaged in a ritual of a release,
impregnated with possibility.

Essence soaked and drenched in passion,
my sweat sanctified your baptism,
christening your early arrival in my womb.

I birthed you in pure ecstasy.

Delivered you front and center
under the shadowy spotlight.

Proud and radiant,
and bold.
Such a glorious sight for all to behold –
I birthed my baby on the dancefloor.

Indigo Magic (for Ntozake Shange)

She walks around with a piece of moon in her pocket.

Cradled gently

in a silk pouch

protected by remnants

of sweet sage

– just in case –

because healing emergencies can come

at any time.

She travels with mystics

who whisper secrets

of Indigo Magic;

cloaking her spirit

in a graceful chrysalis

it's no wonder why she keeps to herself –

she's transforming.

Journeying;

one-step closer to completing

her own rites of passage,

she adorns her womb

in beaded trinkets;

much like the girlhood dolls

she soon grew too old to play with.

But the mischief still erupts wildly in spirit,

visible in giggling eyes

and the slight,

sly

smirk that decorates her face,

subtly hinting

at profound mysteries

and eccentric passions

well beyond imagination.

She's an anomaly.

A child of the universe.

Moon-kissed

and

crowned in glory;

an amethyst astro-projection

from another dimension;

flower petals falling from her aura;

stardust spilling from her lips.

Always protected by the moon in her pocket,

she's blessed
Indigo Magic.

She is. . . Woman

She is
kinetically aesthetic.

Relentless rhythmic energy
expresses her grace of presence,
she's Floetry:
fluid poetry beholden;
a visual ballad of lyrical complexity.
Yet, words fail
to rightfully write in depth,
her beautiful existence.

She is
melodic excellence;
sweet, sensuous synergy in motion.
Surpassing even Beethoven's artistic genius,
she shatters sound waves
and destroys symphonic arrangements
with the subtle structure of her hips.

Silently,

watch

her

walk.

See as she struts nonchalantly yet empowered.

Observe her involuntary tendency to sashay through life

with a sprightly step forward,

marked by an intense focus.

Watch her move –

and see if you don't hear music,

underpinning

and honoring

her very creation

She is:

Woman.

Woman.

Womb man.

Wonder to man.

The womb from which he is birthed;

she is his first teacher,

and her primary leader;

the example of a queen behaviorism embodied.

She is a vessel of supremacy,

God incarnate

embedded in every religious doctrine.
The divine power resides within her temple
as her sacred sex
brings forth the renewals of nations
and yet also threatens its destruction...

She is Kali:
chaotic imbalance.
Thus, lesser mortals fear the throne of pleasure
she possesses,
power beyond measure
and mystery,
underestimated.
She is indescribable,
unrestrained strength.
Deemed dangerous
because she is beyond
simple human comprehension...
She is
Woman.

Woman.
Water.
A welled source of magnitude,
She is Oshun,
river of infinite wisdom
unyielding.

The nourishing element that cultivates the seeds of life.

She is scarlet potency;

rose thorn victory,

stemmed in mystical sacrifice,

she bleeds so you don't have to.

Enduring the pain of a world

that undervalues her worth,

she is wounds unseen;

awe inspiring,

captivating lightening,

she burns defiantly;

a fiery survivor spirit.

She is scarred stories of uniqueness.

Signified in patterned stretch marks

revealing interesting journeys to self-discovery,

she stretches her heart past capacity,

indefinitely

replenishing a love

to redeem a world

that should be kneeling at her feet!

She

is:

Woman.

∞ ∞ ∞

A fountain of me stains the earth...

Crimson tears

flow abundantly

like the river,

I give birth

to infinite possibilities.

New life blossoming

from my bosom

and my womb:

bright,

powerful

and painful,

like the Scarlett letter

emblazoned across my heart;

sacrifice spills freely from my veins

releasing a wave of redemption

for the fallen,

and renewal

for the scorned.

My spirit weeps

willingly

as ordained to

for the world

to begin again.

– *Menstruation*

∞ ∞ ∞

Part 3 - Flower

V. Flower Power & Other Affirmations

I am fearlessly ...

*going after everything that I desire
and everything that I deserve!*

∞∞∞

Journal Entry #8:

What does a completely healthy me look like?

-7 June 2017

∞ ∞ ∞

Journal Entry #9:

I am being proactive in my empowerment, in my own healing.

-14 June 2017

∞ ∞ ∞

Journal Entry #10:

I choose to make the most of every moment.

I choose the moments that bring me the most joy.

<u>I choose to be happy.</u> I choose to embrace the universe and allow the universe to embrace me. I choose to BE.

I will tune into me. Turn up my own frequency to hear my spirit constantly. And I will follow her instructions and guidance.

I choose to honor the spirit.

-21 June 2017

∞∞∞

I Am (Identity Poem)

I am a dreamer!
A believer and practitioner of wishful thinking;
a seeker of enlightenment
pondering my purpose.

I am a fanatic
of the abstract,
chasing ambiguous aspirations,
determined to achieve greatness
– and elusive as that is,
I shall obtain it.

I am focused.
Eyes wide open,
my visions manifest
daily
in fanciful imaginings.
Floating sky high,
living in whimsical,
stargazing dimensions,

I am not of this world;
I am dangerous.

I am a planner;
a doer,
dynamic achiever.
Particularly persistent
and militantly organized
I am
an insufferable
control-freak.
Very precise
in what I want,
how I want it
when I want it –
NOW!

I am impatiently exercising patience.

I find it difficult being idle;
a constant thinker;
Ms. Over-analytical,
I contemplate ideas
I haven't even conceived yet.

I am
a zany

precarious

spirit.

A paradox layered in puzzles

riddled in complexities,

I am

daringly unordinary.

Quirky in my musings,

sometimes

I don't even understand me…

But,

one could never

mislabel me as boring.

I am a diva

of marveled strength.

Ms. Mischievous Goddess,

I am

stubborn,

prideful,

and

overzealous.

Ever relentless in my wrath,

I am

a fearful creature

filled with too much passion –

I

Want

JAIYE EMPRESS

It

ALL...

and I'm

determined to have it.

I am

intimidating,

ambitious,

and

unapologetic

for my intense presence.

I am a child of the universe.

Uncontained by boxes

and boundaries,

my spirit dances freelance

twirling beyond reason

and flirting with ludic sentiment;

I can NOT be tamed.

I am an enigma;

a paradoxical being

desiring anonymity and acceptance.

I crave solitude

and yet

reject it.

172

Searching for peace...

A rueful
romantic cynic,
I am
an eternal optimist
bleeding hopefulness.

A beautiful, bashful butterfly,
I am
an introverted extrovert,
warmly blanketed
in the pensively cold shield
of indifference.

I am
fragile,
tentative
delicateness.

I am creative!

A skillfully, talented Empress,
I am an underrated source
of magic
wielding power unfathomed.

I am
inspiration
and
so
much
more...

I am a work in progress,
striving for greatness
and yet,
I am greatness;
delightful brilliance
shining on high
radiating effortlessly
consistently.
I love
who
I
am,
who
I'm
becoming,
and
who
I have
grown
to be.

I am beautifully ME!

I Am (An Affirmation)

I am healthy

and

a healer.

NOT

too sensitive but intuitive

and compassionate.

I graciously give to the souls that need my gifts.

I love my good spirit,

my open heart,

my optimism.

I am great at introspecting,

adapting to change

and creative expression.

I believe

in the power of affirmations,

positive thinking

and manifestation.

I value
all the joy attainable
that life has to offer.

I am gifted.

I am
Healthy
Holy
A healer.

I am free-spirited,
elevating into my highest form of self.

I am infinite light;
pure energy,
weightless;
beautiful memories of love
bounded by joyful Blackness;
I am
part of the whole.
I am expansive.

I Am A Revolution

I am a revolution.
I am cataclysmic change.

I dismantle antiquated value systems
and disrupt the status quo
simply by living.

Alive and vibrant,
radiating in bold ass,
explosive color,
I'm out here redefining the parameters of possibility,
beautifully
stretching beyond the limitations,
they created for me.

And I do so naturally,
radically.
So much so
that it frightens them:
I cannot be contained.

Nor muted
or shut out.

They love to hate my fearlessness.

I am challenging.
I will challenge you purposely
because that is
who I am.

I transform through touch
telepathically
and kinetically.
Intensely.
I'll force you to shift,
expand,
and grow.

You'll learn to shed
those superficial skins in my presence
or you'll stagnate.

Either way you'll be moved;

the impact of which not easily eradicated
or undone.

I am a revolution.

I am cataclysmic change.

I am the chaos they so consciously shun

and yet secretly yearn for.

I am the excitement they fear,

the stirring they cannot define

control

or escape from.

I am the truth they love to hate.

Goddess Power

I bathe in the essence of Oshun.
Her herbal remedies restore my body,
her scent mixing with my fragrance
to create a memorable signature.

Ma'at governs my sanctuary.
Her laws of morality inscribed
on the walls of my dwelling,
always guiding me on the right path.

I pray to my Ori.
She is the first presence
that wakes me up in the morning
affirming my own personal source of power.

I light a candle to Lakshmi.
She cleanses and purifies my space
opening my heart to the abundant blessings
coming my way.

Yemaya graces my altar.

Balancing the waters of my soul,

she partners with La Luna,

illuminating

the emotional depths worth exploring.

Incarnations of Erzulie stare back at me.

From every corner,

at every angle,

she has made herself comfortable

in the art that adorns my living space.

I am surrounded daily by the divine feminine.

I revere her.

Embrace her.

And I am honored.

Adorning Myself

I smile.
Silently setting my intentions,
peacefully adhering to affirmations
administered by the great ones before me;
lifting my spirit to the heavens
and giving thanks for existence.

I pray.
Meditating in the stillness of beauty,
embracing my joy.
I rub love onto my skin like coconut oil;
its radiance seeping out of my pores
with sensual notes of sage
cedar and Jasmin –
my special scent is blessed.

I speak:
life into healing;
power Into being.
I declare assurance over my purpose

despite not possessing

all of the answers

because I know that anything is possible

and the universe will provide.

I listen.

I write myself telepathic love letters:

soulful reminders to tune inward;

I hear my heartbeat

and remember

my plan:

why I am,

who I am

I am whole.

I honor my presence,

positively pleased I am present

I celebrate ME!

∞ ∞ ∞

Journal Entry #11:

I trust that the universe will provide, and I have faith in me.

- 1 Nov 2017

∞∞∞

Journal Entry #12:

I have the power within me to manifest my own dreams…

I will flow in positivity, love and light, progressing into my best form of self.

- 5 Nov 2017

∞∞∞

Journal Entry #13:

I am purposeful and purpose-filled.

- 19 Nov 2017

∞∞∞

A Haiku

Peace be still in me.

Sunlight beams within my smile.

Life is simple joy.

Soul Flow

My breath is like the ocean.

Deep,
rolling waves of inhalation
flow
to
and from
the source
at its core,
the same essence
escaping and returning to me.

Manifest Destiny

Manifest destiny,
I invite desire to touch every facet of my life.

I engage purposely with the world
to attract all that I deserve.
I am intentional.
Receptive.
Open.
Patient.

I trust the timing of my future,
my blessings are pending.

Today Will Be...
(An Affirmation)

Today will be a day of greatness.

Today will be a day of abundance.

I call forth prosperity.

I radiate feminine energy.

I use my womb

to break the curses

lurking in my subconscious.

My intuition is greater than my fears.

Today will be a day of magic;

a day of opportunities given and granted.

I receive blessings from every direction I turn,

I see bounty everywhere that I look.

I am

several steps closer to my dreams.

I dig deeper

to tap into

a reservoir
of unlimited power,
and I create.

I create my own space of solace.

I carry home with me;
within me.
In my heart
I know
I am worthy.
Deserving.

I deserve love.
I deserve peace.
I deserve joy.

I wholeheartedly embrace my desires
and today,
everyday,
I set myself free.

∞∞∞

Journal Entry #14:

My affirmation card asks me what I need to heal or create in my life. And for me to visualize the response.

I envision a space where I can honor myself. So, I saw myself at home, in my living room, praying, meditating, beading, drinking tea, all of the things I already do with ease and regularity.

That is how I heal or create.

I also saw myself at the beach alive and happy in my own skin. Naked and free.

This is how I heal or create.

I give myself space and time to honor me.

This is how I heal or create.

How I continue to become...

- 24 June 2018

∞∞∞

VI. Fragrant Petals: Nurturing Growth

Journal Entry #15:

I do not wish to be afraid to claim my blessings.

I AM WORTHY.

…

I should know it's okay to be afraid. To change my mind. To get swept away in the moment. To fall down. To make the same mistake twice. To have misguided faith in something that has proven to be a failure. To be naïve and innocent.

I DON'T have all the answers. And the knowledge I do have is tentative. Trial by error. I learn by fucking up over and over again. And that's okay. I may have inadvertently contributed to some of my own pain, but I love me. I love me through every hiccup. Through every malfunction. Every spazzed out moment. Every hard landing and nasty fall. Every breakdown. Every emotional meltdown and over-reaction. I love me through it all.

So, I forgive myself.

I forgive myself for not always being kind to me. For giving everyone else multiple chances but being hesitant to give myself a second one. I forgive myself for being scared. For playing it safe. For being risky, too. For betting it all on a doubtful outcome. I forgive myself for self-doubt. For being too tired sometimes to stick to a goal. For giving up before fully starting.

I forgive myself for it all.

I can do better. I am becoming better.

But I love myself through every step of the process.

I am gentle with me.

- 1 June 2017

∞ ∞ ∞

The Journey

My locs harbor secrets.

Of ancestral wisdom,
modern misgivings
and prophetic fortunes.

If my tresses could talk,
oh goodness, the stories they could tell!
The scandals they would reveal
uncoiled in departed hair cells
stubbornly hanging on by a thread
from my head –
you see,
there are strands of my life
literally entrenched in these locs –
but I don't dare *dread* them...

I draw strength from my mane –
though heavy it is to bear the crown
I lay my burdens down.

Allowing these tendrils to free fall
flowing ever so lovely,
they grace my back
weighty with lessons;
each individual spiral my personal mentor
for experience is the best teacher,
and my locs have seen and been through it all...

Deeply rooted intuition
messily nestles within my follicles
producing impressive new growth –
signifying the Empress's new growth
because I've earned my regality.

Through this spiritual renewal
I achieve a higher elevation of
increased potent vibrancy
each time I shed this dead skin,
my transition into natty freedom
becomes a little less complicated;
and a little more celebrated.

I honor my
lengthy, curly-kinky
emotional scars hanging loose,
as stunning testimonials;
delicately resilient

and different.

You see,
my locs can't help
but to call attention to themselves!

They're visible whispers of mute memories;
confessions of self-discovery
professing to those close enough to see:
my beauty comes with a price.

Metamorphosis

Like a tree shedding its leaves
my inner fruit blossoms to prime peakness.

Bearing a soulful ripening,
ready to showcase the marvelous,
colorful layers of the growth I sowed from so long ago,
I let my rooted treasures go.

Fragile petals wafting sublimely in the wind
indicate the conclusion of a season,
as I start anew.

Sacrificing superficial attachments
to material memories
extending longer than necessary,
it has been past due time
to prune these weeds…

Shedding external skins,
I step into a new transition;

beautiful butterfly living

flying into new horizons,

the possibilities produced by the past pain

prompts an evolving ascension;

vibrating higher...

Departing from vanity,

my inner joy radiates more outwardly

than the crown I often took for granted;

and so it is removed.

Unlike the strength sapped from Sampson,

I felt relief the moment the weight fell from my head.

Unburdened of the 140 tales spun unraveled
from Rumplestiltskin's spindle,

reality dissolves into surrealism,

but now I truly see me again:

real,

raw and vividly.

The journey continues.

Metamorphosis.

Meditation

I sat in silence before the dancing flame

embracing myself;

holding myself fiercely,

whispering to me,

"I forgive you."

And I was made whole again.

Soul Work

Tear stained smile;
crystal laced aura,
scented with oils
rising to greet the dawn of day –
this is soul work.

Healing Is A Cycle

Healing is a cycle,
I'm reminded when my heart feels heavy
compressed by too many memories
overwhelmed with too much emotion.

I know these feelings are fleeting.

They ebb and flow
following the tempo of change,
keeping pace with life's erratic rhythms.

But it doesn't mean the hurt
doesn't echo just as loudly in the background,
resounding deep into the recesses of my soul.

I wish
I could mute
or
pause
this part in my growth's succession.

Or skip past to the better parts in the series.

But healing is a spiral.

So, I'm cycling through
around and beyond
past ailments
and present misgivings
to relearn lessons
I thought I heeded,
returning to moments
I desperately wish to bypass
yet,
these remembrances are needed;
and, so too,
is the reflection.

I'm reminded of how far I've come
and what work there is
still left to be done.
I know
this journey
wasn't meant to be easy
or fun
or pretty
or enjoyable
most days.

But it's worth it.
And I'm committed.

My healing is inevitable.

$\mathcal{S}$cars

Jagged memories;
half healed
keloid thoughts
that still throb when it rains.

Cocoa and shea butters
only add a layer of sheen
to the crooked edges of my heart.

But I beautify them anyways
because
unsightly as they may be,
my scars speak
a glorious truth,
unapologetically
sharing pieces
of my story
vividly.

So, I show them off with pride,

displaying to the world

all those times

where I

actually

lived.

Self-Care

So,
I've decided
to be more active
in my own courtship.

I've scheduled calendar appointments
complete with alarmed reminders
to specifically set aside time
solely,
especially
for me.

I've made lists of places I have longed to visit
just as soon as I found the time to spare,
to share
with the right person
in the right moment,
only to never go.

Best made plans to prioritize me

get postponed,
cancelled,
or flat out neglected;
a dream deferred
time and time again.

But that was then.

My Saturday night agenda
is already circled
with my upcoming self-date.

The reservation for one
saved and set;
internal clock preprogrammed to
'Do Not Disturb'
I excitedly look forward to fully
romanticizing me.

Finally!

I'll have a reason
to tell the world
NO!
I can't.
I won't.
I don't want to.

I'm busy.

Grounded

She smelled like the Earth:
grounded,
sturdy,
dependable.
Memorable,
like red clay,
she seemed to stick to you
in all the hard to reach places;
her stains impossible to wash off.

She smelled like fragrant dirt:
ancient,
strong;
everywhere and nowhere;
deep resin wisdom
rooted in time immemorial.

She clung to you when least expected
and made you remember to respect the
not so beautiful parts residing inside of you.

She smelled like the Earth:
powerful,
bountiful,
immovable,
hurt.

Perspective

"Recharge, renew, respond."

I collect the broken pieces
of my shattered world
and build a makeshift nest.

I burrow there
in my hastily crafted safe space
and rest.

Meditative reflections remind me:
the worst is not the end
and the "end"
will begin again
tomorrow.

Therefore, it can all wait.

"Renew, recharge, then respond."

∞∞∞

Cry.

Thrive.

Repeat.

And if all else fails,

make a cup of tea

- Steps for Healing

∞ ∞ ∞

(My) Loneliness

I'm learning to sit with it;
to befriend it.

I don't fear its name the way I used to.

I'm learning to embrace it;
to not dread
its sudden appearance
or its persistent presence.

Because sometimes
it overstays its welcome.

Though "welcome" is being generous
since it often drops by
unannounced.

But still,
we converse
from time to time

and it's not this menacing,

harrowing

thing.

Though it can be

quite heavy;

I'm learning how

to view it as less of a burden.

Dreams

When I was a child,
I said I'd be the first Black woman president;
or maybe a basketball player in the WNBA;
or a singer;
famous writer;
or poet.

I was hella shy though.

My dreams were creative
and ambitious
and daring.

I didn't give up my presidential dreams until I was seventeen.

Now I dream of legacy building.

Of being a mother;
of family rearing and raising;
of radical loving partnerships;

of changing the world

one poem at a time;

of

writing my fears away

to a nonexistent place

when they threaten to overwhelm my dreaming

to the point where I don't want to do so anymore

Because it hurts

to imagine

that one day

I'll have to give them up again –

like when I was seventeen,

realizing that certain things are just out of reach,

and not all dreams

come true…

∞∞∞

Journal Entry #16:

The universe listens... but I don't always.

I'm working on that.

Everyday my intuition grows stronger and whether I allow her to or not, she speaks. I just need to do a better job of paying attention to her. And to stop negotiating. I keep compromising like my way has yielded the results I want.

Why won't I trust the process?

Why do I keep backing out of my own happiness? Sabotaging it, thinking it will lead me to much greater instead of truly allowing it to happen?

I asked my future self am I happy?

And she told me, yes you are.

You are happy and loved.

I am happy and loved!

- 28 Sep 2017

∞∞∞

VII. Flowered Fierceness (As the petals unfold...)

Journal Entry #17:

What is my definition of success?

What does it mean to be successful?

Success to me is making a positive impact, wherever I go, on as many people as possible.

It's loving wholeheartedly: myself, life, the people that matter to me. It's choosing the best for myself, not settling.

Success is being an amazing wife and mother.

It's creating a beautiful legacy that those after me will be inspired to continue.

It's finishing what I started. Manifesting my dreams, no matter how abstract or impossible they may seem initially.

Success is staying true to me no matter what!

- 28 Sep 2017

∞∞∞

Sexy is a state of being!

*It took me awhile to get comfortable
in my own skin, to show off the
different parts of me without fear.*

Now I embrace me wholeheartedly.

I enjoy the way I feel,

the way I move,

the way I look in this body!

My attitude is sexy.

Self-confidence is the allure I exude,

and I love how it smells on me!

∞∞∞

Sexy

Sexy
is her namesake,
and also
she signature scent.

Exuding an allure of attitude,
diva potency
wafts from her pores
as perfumed petals of pride
leave vivacious trails
of fragrant seduction
softly billowing behind her;
the impression lasting long after
she exits.

She's a Siren.

Magnificently owning her power
and embracing her love design
like she's destined to.

I love the way she moves,
the way she laughs
and how she carries herself;
the way she looks
so well at ease in her own skin –

I love the smell of her confidence.

Scurrying

Safety is an illusion.

Nothing is guaranteed
except change
and I do not run from it.
I no longer scurry for protection,

I

am

protected

in my own stance;

in my stride

of badassness.

I own my own attitude.

Practicing radical acceptance
of my scars,
the lessons...
No more running.

No more scurrying.

I stride with purpose.

Stride

Strut in your sexy,
dear queen.

Hold your head up high
because you've been low.

You deserve to stand tall,
taller than the bullshit
that has stood stacked against you.

Strut
in your sexy,
dear queen.

Step deliberate
and
with purpose
into your limelight.

This

is

your

moment.

Own it!

∞∞∞

Journal Entry #18:

My dreams are not just mine. They are for those who have ceased dreaming. Who cannot dream any longer. I want to honor those souls who had unfinished dreams and potential purposes. I owe it to those who came before, and those who left prematurely to finish what I start, and to complete it to the best of my abilities.

*Iono, if this is morbid but it's part of my motivation. I could not be here. And for a brief moment, **I didn't want to be here**.*

But I am. And I'm glad.

And I won't take my being here for granted.

- 18 Mar 2018

∞∞∞

Yemoja

She kisses my womb.

Her salty breath hovers near my skin
whispering secrets
of infinite wisdom.

I am held
in the immeasurable depths
of her watery bosom,
replenished,
nourished,
and sustained with new life,
new possibilities.

She welcomes me home to a peace
present in me all along.

She reminds me,
she has been here with me all along.

Closer

Ascension.

Motion.

Gaining momentum.

Higher.

Velocity.

Elevating.

Higher.

Floating weightless –

if I could just let these burdens go.

Free-falling.

Lighter,

faster,

higher.

Flying higher

and

higher.

Away from these fears;

these doubts;

these tears;

these chains

that shackle;
keep me grounded.
Higher motion.
Elevation.
Evolution.
Growth.

Audacity

Wildflower,
Indigo woman,
how dare you thrive?

How dare you take up space?
How dare you live out loud
boisterous and proud
defying the chains
graciously given to you?

How dare you shapeshift at will?
How dare you create new spaces to fill?

How dare you revel
in the spotlight
astonishing the world
when all eyes are upon you?

How dare you stand your ground?
How dare you kiss the sky?

How dare you disrupt daily normalcy
with your magic
casting spells
at random
spilling rapture everywhere?

How dare you rewrite all the rules?
How dare you assert
your right to choose?

How dare you grow?

How dare you be...
who you are?

How dare you,
Wildflower,
Indigo woman –
How dare you *not*?

∞ ∞ ∞

Journal Entry # 19:

This last year has been a testament that somewhere along the way, I lost myself. And I've been struggling to not only find myself, but keep myself.

I want to do a better job of keeping myself in the future...

- 27 July 2018

∞∞∞

I lived!

I cried,

I thrived,

I fought,

I bled,

I triumphed and then repeated
the cycle all over again.

Here is living proof that **<u>I LIVED!</u>**

∞∞∞

A Message of Gratitude

True story: writing my acknowledgements was one of the hardest tasks I had to complete.

I felt thwarted by the universe as I wrote and rewrote heartfelt words, only to have lost them in the ether of cyberspace.

So, finally, I decided to take a different approach.
I had a list of names of people I didn't want to forget to include and then I hesitated over those relationships that greatly impacted me and the development of this book but were no longer part of my life. And the more I contemplated, the more I delayed writing these words and ultimately releasing my story. I wanted everything to be perfect.

And maybe that's why my first couple of attempts were lost, because while they were authentic, the intent was misguided.

Therefore, I want to extend my deepest gratitude to the collective community of interactions, experiences and people that have blessed my life thus far.
A special shout out to my first loves:

Linda "Mama Bear," and Clint "Boi Boi" Singletary, you are the absolute best Trifecta family ever!

Thank you for your incessant encouragement, support, love, laughs, and so much more. You always inspire me to be the best sister, daughter, and person I can be…and you only mildly jones on me when I fall short!

I'm so thankful to be part of this special Trifecta trinity. Y'all are truly the best parts of me.

I love you so much!

To my dad, Timothy Laurence Singletary: there are so many things I wish we hadn't left unsaid; so many moments lost for us both. But I still feel you and I carry you with me always. My legacy will be that much greater because of the impact you have made on my life!

One day, I will have the courage to tell you everything that has been on my heart to say...but somehow, I believe you already know. I love and miss you dearly.

To my special soul sistren:

Krystin aka "Cruel" Mack, Amelia "Anime" Kyles, I appreciate the sisterhood each of you have gifted me. Thank you for going beyond the realms of friendship to become part of my family.

For those who mean a great deal to me, that I haven't named, I hope I do a well enough job in our personal encounters of expressing my appreciation of you and your gifts, so that you _know_ your importance and how integral you have been in the development of my story.

I love you and I hope that is evident in everyday life.

To my extensive family, friends, mentors, fellow artists, soul tribe members, community advocates, allies and more, thank you for believing, supporting, encouraging and sharing in my craft.

I hope you see aspects of yourself in my words because you have inspired and impacted me in more ways than you know.

Thank you.

Jasmin "Jaiye Empress" Singletary

About The Author

Jaiye Empress

Jaiye Empress is the self-described "Love Poetess," and "G.R.I.O.T.-Soul Seer."

G.R.I.O.T stands for:
Goddess. Rebel. Inspiring. Original. Thought.

Jaiye uses poetry and artistic storytelling to share soul stirring chronicles about love, Black womxnhood, and self-spiritual journeys. Her aim is to inspire the receivers of her words to conduct their own personal soul audits in order to feel whole, healthy and joyous.

Jaiye is also the founder and owner of Empressive Expressions, a premium art, beauty and edutainment company that celebrates Black femininity.
From this platform, Jaiye creates spaces and products that affirm and empower Black girls and womxn through the art of self expression.

At Empressive Empressions, every product is a poem, every

poem tells a story and every story told, speaks from the soul!

https://www.everythingempressive.com
https://www.facebook.com/empressivexpressions
https://www.instagram.com/empressive_expressions

www.ingramcontent.com/pod-product-compliance
Lightning Source LLC
Chambersburg PA
CBHW031947090426
42739CB00006B/114